Fun with Addition

Katie Peters

Lerner Publications ◆ Minneapolis

Lerner Publications
An imprint of Lerner Publishing Group, Inc.
241 First Avenue North
Minneapolis, MN 55401 USA

For reading levels and more information, look up this title at www.lernerbooks.com.

Main body text set in Memphis Pro 24/39
Typeface provided by Linotype.

Photo Acknowledgments
The images in this book are used with the permission of: © demidoff/Shutterstock Images, pp. 3, 12, 16 (center, right); © fizkes/Shutterstock Images, pp. 4–5; © SViktoria/Shutterstock Images, pp. 6–7; © Belle Ciezak/Shutterstock Images, pp. 8–9, 16 (left); © Daria Medvedeva/Shutterstock Images, pp. 10–11; © Liudmyla Matviiets/Shutterstock Images, p. 13 (numbers); © Irina Wilhauk/Shutterstock Images, pp. 14–15.

Front Cover: © demidoff/Shutterstock Images

Library of Congress Cataloging-in-Publication Data

Names: Peters, Katie, author.
Title: Fun with addition / Katie Peters.
Description: Minneapolis, MN, USA : Lerner Publications Company, an imprint of Lerner Publishing Group, Inc., [2024] | Series: Math all around. Pull ahead readers - nonfiction | Includes index. | Audience: Ages 4–7 | Audience: Grades K–1 | Summary: "Young readers will enjoy learning how to add using this nonfiction book. Engaging photographs and easy-to-read text help make addition fun! Pairs with the fiction text Saving Up"—Provided by publisher.
Identifiers: LCCN 2023002299 (print) | LCCN 2023002300 (ebook) | ISBN 9798765608654 (lib. bdg.) | ISBN 9798765616147 (epub)
Subjects: LCSH: Addition—Juvenile literature.
Classification: LCC QA115 .P468 2024 (print) | LCC QA115 (ebook) | DDC 513.2/11—dc23/eng/20230519

LC record available at https://lccn.loc.gov/2023002299
LC ebook record available at https://lccn.loc.gov/2023002300

Manufactured in the United States of America
1 – CG – 12/15/23

Table of Contents

Fun with Addition

I can add. To add means
to join together.

I have three cars.

I have two cars.

Together we have five cars.

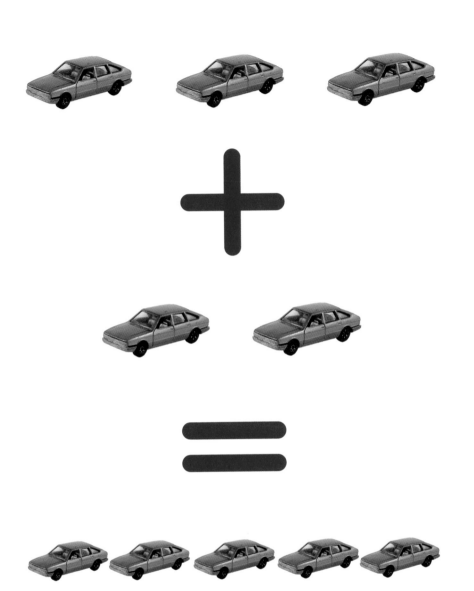

$$3+2=5$$

Three plus two equals five.

Can you add?

Did You See It?

car

three

two

Index